Books and Games

ELDONNA L. EVERTTS
Language Arts

LYMAN C. HUNT
Reading

BERNARD J. WEISS
Linguistics and Curriculum

Edited by Jane Berkowitz and Craig Bettinger

Educational Consultants: Patsy Montague and Janet Sprout

THE HOLT BASIC READING SYSTEM · LEVEL 4 ·

HOLT, RINEHART AND WINSTON, INC.
New York / Toronto / London / Sydney

ACKNOWLEDGMENTS

Grateful acknowledgment is given to the following authors and publishers:

Harcourt Brace Jovanovich, Inc., for "Picture People" from *Whispers and Other Poems*. Copyright © 1958 by Myra Cohn Livingston. Reprinted by permission of Harcourt Brace Jovanovich, Inc.

Highlights for Children, for "My Dog" by Marguerite Hamilton from *Children's Activities*. Used by permission of Highlights for Children, Inc., Columbus, Ohio.

Instructor Publications, Inc., for "Shopping" by Josephine van Dolzen Pease from *The Instructor*. Used by permission of The Instructor Publications, Inc.

ILLUSTRATED BY

Ray Cruz, pages 4–5
Eleanor Mill, pages 6–25, 33–40, 42–59
Lionel Kalish, pages 26–30, 60–61
Tim and Greg Hildebrandt, pages 31, 62–63
Viewpoint Graphics, Inc., page 32
Marilyn Bass Goldman, page 41

ISBN 0-03-082851-1
3456789 071 9876543

Contents

4

Picture People

I like to peek

inside a book

where all the picture people look.

I like to peek

at them and see

if they are peeking back at me.

—Myra Cohn Livingston

A Game Book

Ben sees a game book.

Ben reads the book.

Ben sees a game for one.

Ben plays the game.

Dan comes into the house.

Dan and Ben read the book.

The boys see a game for two.

The two boys play the game.

Jim comes into the house.

Jim and Dan and Ben read the book.

The boys see a game for three.

The three boys play the game.

Jim says, "Good-by."

Dan and Ben play.

The boys play the game for two.

Dan says, "Good-by."

Ben plays a game.

14

The game is for one.

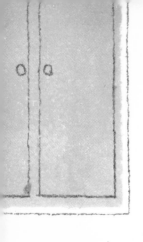

The Cookbook

Jenny and Jill are in the house.

Jenny is the big girl.

Jill is the little girl.

16

Jenny and Jill see a cookbook.

The girls open the book.

Jenny reads the book.

The girls see cookies in the cookbook.

Jenny likes cookies.

Jill likes cookies.

Jenny reads the cookbook.

The girls make the cookies.

The cookies go in.

And the cookies come out.

The cookies go in.

And the cookies come out.

M-m-m! The cookies are good!

Candy

Make some peanut butter candy.

You need

    1 cup peanut butter

    1 cup corn syrup

    1¼ cups powdered milk

    1¼ cups powdered sugar

First mix it.

Roll it into little balls.

Then eat it.

Labels visible in illustration: CORN SYRUP, POWDERED MILK, PEANUT BUTTER, POWDERED SUGAR

Read the Sign!

Where do you go?

Read the sign!

The sign tells where to go.

What do you do?

Read the sign!

The sign tells what to do.

What is it?

Read the sign!

The sign tells what it is.

Who is here?

Read the sign!

The sign tells who is here.

DR. COOK
D.D.S.

A sign tells **where**.

A sign tells **what**.

A sign tells **who**.

30

Stringing Words

A bear makes **cookies**.

The	boy	makes	**games.**
A	girl	sees	**cookies.**
One	bear	likes	**books.**

The	boys	make	**games.**
Two	girls	see	**cookies.**
Some	bears	like	**books.**

31

Sentence Patterns. Let the children choose a red word, a blue word, a gray word, and a black word to form a sentence.

Making Words

DAN

D an

c an

c an

J an

J an

r an

r an

p an

Initial Consonant Substitution. Have the first word read. Point out that the girl is changing the first letter. Have the new word read. Continue with the remaining words.

Rex

"Here, Rex," said Dan.

"Come and see the dog book."

34

"Here is a good trick," said Dan.

"Come and see the trick.

Come out here, Rex.

Do the trick!"

Rex did come out.

Rex did not do the trick.

"Here, Rex!

Good boy," said Dan.

"Do the trick!"

37

Rex did not do the trick.

"You are not a trick dog," said Dan.

"Come into the house, Rex."

Rex did not go in.
Rex did the trick!

My Dog

My dog is lots of company
When I am all alone,
But he is too much company
When I have an ice cream cone!

—Marguerite Hamilton

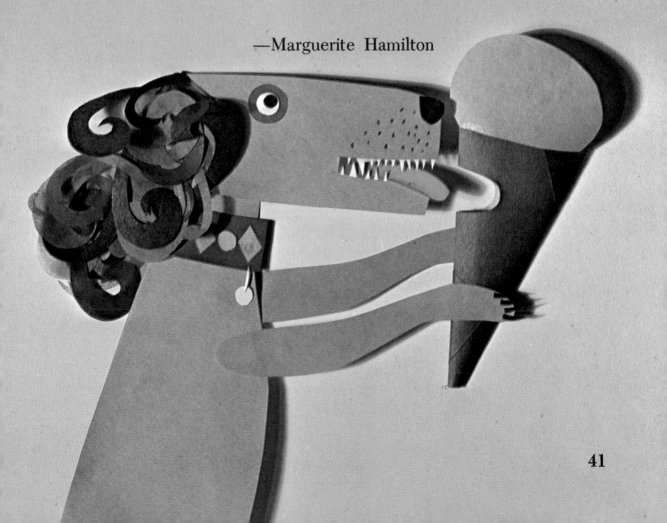

Find the Cookies

The boys and girls play a game.

The game is "Find the Cookies."

Two boys see a big sign.

The sign says, "Go into the house."

Go into
the house.

43

The boys and girls go into the house.

They see a little sign.

The sign says, "Find Rex."

The boys and girls find Rex.

And they see a sign.

The sign says, "Find a blue book."

The boys and girls find some books.

They see the blue book.

A sign is in the book.

The sign says, "Find a big book."

Jill sees the big book.

She sees a sign in the book.

The sign says, "Find a blue pig."

"A blue pig!" says Jill.

"Here is a blue pig," says Ben.

"Come in here.

Come and see the pig."

The boys and girls see the pig.

Where are the cookies?

In the pig!

The Big Store

Three boys go to the big store.

They go to find books.

The boys see two signs.

The big boy reads the In sign.

Dan and the big boy go in.

Ben sees the Out sign.

Ben goes in.

"Read the signs, Ben," says Dan.

"Go in where you see the In sign.

Go out where you see the Out sign."

The boys are in the store.

They see two signs.

One sign says, "Up."

One sign says, "Down."

Dan and the big boy go up.

And Ben goes down.

"Come here, Ben," says Dan.

"The books are up here.

Read the signs.

Find the Up sign and come up."

Ben sees the Up sign.

Ben goes up.

The boys find the books.

They see the Down sign.

The big boy goes down.

Dan goes down.

And Ben goes down.

The boys see the Out sign.

The big boy goes out.

Dan goes out.

And Ben goes out.

Shopping

I like to hop,
    and I like to skip,
And I like to go
    on a shopping trip.

60

I like to stand
   by the bookman's shelf
And choose a book
   all by myself.

—Josephine van Dolzen Pease

61

Help the Kitten Get Down

make

cake

rake

bake

lake

fake

Jake

Initial Consonant Substitution. Let the children take turns trying to get the kitten by reading down the word ladder.

Stringing Words

Ben		Jenny	make	cookies.
Dan	and	Jill	find	signs.
Jim		Rex	see	games.

Did Ben and Jenny see cookies?

Do	Ben		Jenny	make	cookies?
Did	Dan	and	Jill	find	signs?
	Jim		Rex	see	games?

Sentence Patterns. Have the children choose a word from each column to form sentences.

63

New Words

The words listed beside the page numbers below are introduced in *Books and Games,* Level 4 in THE HOLT BASIC READING SYSTEM.

6.	game	20.	go	35.	trick
	Ben	21.	out	36.	did
7.	plays	23.	good		not
8.	Dan	26.	sign	42.	find
	into		tells	44.	they
10.	Jim		to	47.	pig
12.	says	27.	what	52.	store
16.	cookbook	28.	it	53.	signs
	Jenny	33.	Rex		goes
	Jill	34.	said	55.	up
18.	cookies		dog		down
19.	make				